Raspberry Pi

A Step-by-Step Guide for Beginners to Learn All the Essentials of Raspberry Pi and Create Simple Hardware Projects Like an Arcade Box or Turning Your Device Into a Phone

Julian James McKinnon

Table of Contents

Raspberry Pi 1
Table of Contents 2
Introduction 5
Chapter 1: What is Raspberry Pi 8

    The Specifications You Need to Know 11
    Are There Different Versions of Raspberry Pi? 13
    The Raspberry Pi Operating System 18
    A Quick Look at Raspbian 21
    Why Should I Choose to Work with Raspberry Pi? 24

Chapter 2: Setting Up the Raspberry Pi 33

    Things to Know to Get Started in Raspberry Pi 35
    How to Install the Operating System 38
    How to Hook Up Our Raspberry Pi Device 42
    Setting Up Raspbian 43
    How to Configure the Raspberry Pi 46
    Connecting the Raspberry Pi to Your Home Wi-Fi 48
    Connecting to the Bluetooth Devices 50
    Connecting to Raspberry Pi Remotely 52

Chapter 3: How to Navigate Through the Raspberry Pi 55

    The Important Files in Raspberry Pi 56
    How to Navigate the Desktop Environment Menus 59
    Writing Code in Your Console 68
    Writing Code in a New Document 70
    How to Write Python Comments 72
    Basic Patterns in Python 75
    Handling Our Regular Expressions 78
    A Look at the Loops 80
    Handling Your Inheritances 90

Chapter 5: How to Use the Raspberry PI 95

How to Interface Our Electronics 95
Understanding Communication Protocols 99
Doing Some Real-Time Interfacing with Arduino 101
How to Capture Videos, and Images 104
How to Record and Play Audio 108

Chapter 6: Learning About the GPIO Pins on This Device 112

Chapter 7: Easy Ways to Troubleshoot the Raspberry Pi 118

How to Avoid a Corrupted SD Card 120
Checking the Cables You Use 124

Chapter 8: Simple Projects to Work within Raspberry Pi 128

The Arcade Box 129
Turning the Device Into a Phone 134

Conclusion 140

© **Copyright 2020 - All rights reserved.**
The content contained within this book may not be reproduced, duplicated or transmitted without direct written permission from the author or the publisher.
Under no circumstances will any blame or legal responsibility be held against the publisher, or author, for any damages, reparation, or monetary loss due to the information contained within this book. Either directly or indirectly.

Legal Notice:

This book is copyright protected. This book is only for personal use. You cannot amend, distribute, sell, use, quote or paraphrase any part, or the content within this book, without the consent of the author or publisher.

Disclaimer Notice:

Please note the information contained within this document is for educational and entertainment purposes only. All effort has been executed to present accurate, up to date, and reliable, complete information. No warranties of any kind are declared or implied. Readers acknowledge that the author is not engaging in the rendering of legal, financial, medical or professional advice. The content within this book has been derived from various sources. Please consult a licensed professional before attempting any techniques outlined in this book.

By reading this document, the reader agrees that under no circumstances is the author responsible for any losses, direct or indirect, which are incurred as a result of the use of the information contained within this document, including, but not limited to, — errors, omissions, or inaccuracies.

Introduction

Congratulations on purchasing **Raspberry Pi,** aond thank you for doing so.

The following chapters will discuss all of the different parts that we need to work with when it comes to the Raspberry Pi device.

This is the perfect device for any developer to work with, and if you learn how to use it in the proper manner, you will find that it can help you get your feet wet and make it easier for you to really jump in and see some results with your own programming skills.

In this guidebook, we are going to take some time to explore what we are able to do with the Raspberry Pi, and some of the reasons that it is such a beneficial program to learn how to work with.

We will start out with a nice introduction to what the Raspberry Pi is all about, along with some of the history of where this board came from and how we are meant to use it.

We will also spend some of our time looking at the various benefits that come with this device to help us get started.

From there, it is time to get into the nitty-gritty of what we are able to do with this kind of device.

We are going to look at some of the steps that we can take in order to get this device set up in our own homes, such as getting the operating system to work on here, configuring the device, and even how to connect this to the wi-fi in our homes and to other Bluetooth devices if that is what we choose to do.

When we are done with that, it is time for us to move on to some of the navigation that has to happen to ensure that we are going to get this device to behave in the way that we want including how to navigate through all of the files, folders, and menus.

This is where we will need to spend some time taking a look at how to work with the Python coding language.

There are other languages that work with the Raspberry Pi if you would like to use them, but for a beginner who has never been able to do much with coding and programming, Python is one of the best options to go with.

This guidebook will talk about some of the options when it comes to using the Python IDLE, and then we will look again at some of the basics that we need to explore when it comes to working with the Python code and writing some of our own along the way.

The next topic that we need to spend some time on is how to use the Raspberry Pi for some of our own programming needs.

We will look at some of the communication protocols and how to do some of the interfacings that we want with the Raspberry Pi device and other devices of our choice.

We can then spend a bit of time looking at how to work with the GPIO pins on this device and what each one means, before moving on to some of the tips and tricks that all beginner programmers need to know in order to get the most out of this device for their own needs.

There are a lot of things that we need to keep in mind and understand when it is time to do some of the work that we want in programming.

But the Raspberry Pi device is one of the best options that we can work with when we are ready to get started, and we want to ensure that this is all going to work in the manner that our coding and application models need.

When you are ready to learn more about how to work with the Raspberry Pi device, and how to code with Python so you can really get this device to work well, make sure to check out this guidebook to help you get started.

There are plenty of books on this subject on the market, thanks again for choosing this one!

Every effort was made to ensure it is full of as much useful information as possible; please enjoy it!

Chapter 1: What is Raspberry Pi

There are going to be a lot of really cool things that we are able to find in the world of technology today.

We are able to find a lot of different programming languages to work with to write codes and a lot of tools and accessories that sneak in and help us get things done as well.

With all of this technology growing and changing all of the time, sometimes, this is going to make beginners feel like they are too far behind and that they should just give up rather than trying.

They worry that the work is going to be too hard for them to get it done.

The neat thing here is that Raspberry Pi is going to be there in order to help to solve this problem.

This is going to be a small computer board, which is about the size of a credit card, that is able to hook up to the computer monitor or your TV.

It is going to be smaller in size, but it will have a lot of power with it and can provide people of all ages and experience levels with ways to explore how the world of computers work, and can make it easier to learn how to work with a variety of programming languages, whether we are looking at the Python language, C++, and Scratch.

Compared to some of the other methods of learning to program out there, this one is going to be a lot easier to work with.

It is going to be easier than most of the other tools for programming out there, and it is going to provide us with a safe way to learn and practice our skills, even as a beginner.

To start here, the Raspberry Pi device is going to be anything that we would expect our traditional desktop computer to do, such as processing different voices, searching online, creating tables, doing gaming, playing videos in HD, and more.

Even more than this, we will find that this device also comes with the ability to interact with the world outside as well.

There have been a lot of different projects in a digital manner that can be made with this device.

This can include homes with birds that have cameras on them, meteorological stations, and even detectors that parents are able to work with.

As you can see, there is actually quite a bit that we need to know when it is time to work with Raspberry Pi, and you will be able to utilize it for a lot of the different projects that are out there.

We are going to take a look at some of the options that are out there for this device, and we will learn some of the coding that is necessary in order to get it started.

It is amazing what we are able to do when it comes to working with the Raspberry Pi.

It is such a simple device that we can work with, but it really does make the difference when it comes to how well we are able to learn about and work with computers and even how we are able to work through the process of learning new coding and programming language.

The Specifications You Need to Know

The next thing that we need to take a look at here is some of the specifications that we need to know when it comes to working with the Raspberry Pi.

This is going to be a little bit different than what we are used to seeing with some of the other devices that we may want to work with, but you will find that it is going to work in the manner that you want.

Some of the specifications that you need to know about for this will be talked about in this section:

Even though the Raspberry Pi 3 is a smaller device, there are a lot of components present that you will enjoy with this small computer.

The Raspberry Pi 3 is the third generation of Raspberry Pi, and the main differences that you are going to see with this version compared to the older versions include:

1. 1.2 GHz 64-bit quad-core ARMv8 CPU
2. 802.11n Wireless LAN
3. Bluetooth 4.1
4. Bluetooth Low Energy

In addition to some of the changes between Raspberry Pi 3 and the earlier versions, there are a few other components that you are going to enjoy when you use this product.

These include:

1. VideoCore IV 3D graphics core
2. Micro SD card slot
3. Display interface
4. Camera interface
5. Combined 3.5-mm audio jack with composite video
6. Ethernet port
7. Full HDMI port
8. 40 GPIO pins
9. 4 USB ports
10. 1 GB RAM

Are There Different Versions of Raspberry Pi?

The next thing that we need to take a look at is whether there are a few different versions of the Raspberry Pi program that we are able to work with.

The cool thing is that there are many versions, and the one that you want to work with is going to depend on the projects that you want to finish, and your overall goals.

Right now, Raspberry Pi 3 is seen as the newest version of this programming choice, and it is going to be able to handle some of the more advanced kinds of programming that you would like to do.

There are also some other options and models that bring in some new features that you can rely on as well. Some of the different versions and types of Raspberry Pi that a programmer is able to work with include:

- Raspberry PI 1 Model A:

  This Model A version is the original that came out in 2012.

  The Plus version of this came out a few years later and was an improvement because it had a larger hard drive, and the price point came in lower than the previous version.

Raspberry Pi 2 Model B:

The first generation of this came out in 2012, and then the Plus model came out in 2014.

The Plus version of the Model B came in with a lower price, and it allowed the user to work with a microSD slot rather than relying on the standard SD slot that was in previous versions.

- Raspberry Pi Zero:

This model of the Raspberry Pi family came out in 2015.

The Zero was designed to be smaller than some of the other versions, and this resulted in reduced output and input for the user.

However, it is the least expensive of the Raspberry Pi's, which made it more affordable than ever.

When the Zero originally came out, it didn't have any video input options.

But in 2016, there was a second version of this released that had this feature.

- Raspberry Pi 2:

This is the model that has a lot more features compared to any of the models that came out before.

It was released in early 2015, and the model is considered one of the higher-end versions of this family.

Even though it is higher-end, it is still very affordable, coming in at just $35.

- Raspberry Pi 3:

    This is the newest model of this computer family.

    It was released in early 2016, and it comes bundled with all the additions that you need in order to really get things going with this computer.

    Some of the accessories that are often sold with this model include USB boot capabilities, Bluetooth, and Wi-Fi.

Keep in mind that these are just a few of the different options that you are able to choose to work with when it comes to the Raspberry Pi program.

Even though you are able to pick out a few options to make it work, you will find that all of them do have a few features that are pretty standard.

For example, you are going to quickly notice that all of them are going to come with the Broadcom feature on a chip, and then the central processing system that they rely on is going to have the protocol of ARM.

There is also a GPU found on all of the versions of the system.

Every board is going to also have a slot present for at least one USB. Often more, though, some of them do come with two, three, and even four slots that we can rely on based on our needs.

You will also find that there are other slots on your device that are meant for the phone jacks, HDMI, and composite video output to help if you want to do some work with the audio on some of these projects as well.

The good thing that you are going to see here is that the team who worked here to create and develop a lot of the models that come with Raspberry Pi are going to also be in charge of the Raspbian operating system as well, which is going to be a great operating system to help us get more out of the system.

This operating system is going to be similar to what we are able to find when working with Linux, so if you have used that operating system in the past, you are going to find that the Raspbian operating system is going to feel pretty familiar here.

Another thing to notice here is that when you work with the Raspberry Pi, you will then be able to work with a few other operating systems as well.

This system is going to handle other systems like RISC OS, Ubuntu, and Windows, and often Linux works well on it too.

So, you are able to go through and pick out the one that works the best for your own needs along the way.

The Raspberry Pi Operating System

To make sure that we are able to get the Raspberry Pi device up and running in the manner that we would like, and to ensure that it is going to be usable, there has to be one of the operating systems in place.

This can be a bit scary to work with if you are not sure of the steps to take, the best approach is to pick out some kind of operating system that is going to suit whatever tasks that you would use the Raspberry Pi for in the first place.

One of the things that you may be a bit surprised about when you first get started here is that there are many coding languages and operating systems that actually work on this device, so you have a lot of choices on what you would like to do with this one.

You need to go through and pick out the option that you like the best, but some of the best options that work well with this kind of device include:

1. Raspbian:

    This is the official operating system that is supported by this device.

    This is a simple operating system to work with, and if you do not have a preference for one of the other options or you have never worked with one before, you will find that this can be a great option to handle.

2. Pidora:

    This is a Fedora Remix operating system that has been changed a bit, so it works well with Raspberry Pi.

3. RaspBMC:

    This is a free and open-sourced media center.

    If you plan to use the device just for that, then this is a good operating system to choose from.

4. OpenELEC:

    This is a Linux based operating system that is a bit smaller, so it works better on the device.

    It is able to turn your Raspberry Pi into a Kodi media center.

5. RISC OS:

    This is an operating system that is very compact, which makes it fast.

    This one has been designed in a way that works the best on devices with ARM architecture.

6. Arch:

This is going to be a flexible and lightweight Linux distribution that you can work with.

7. Python:

   Python is one of the best programming languages that you can work with as a beginner.

   We will take a look at some of the coding that you should know about when it comes to using Python so you can write your own codes on this device.

A Quick Look at Raspbian

While we are here, we need to take a closer look at how we can work with the Raspbian operating system.

There are other options that we can go with, but none are going to provide us with the information and the ease of use to work with the Raspberry Pi as we are going to find with the Raspbian operating system.

This is a good operating system that we can work with, and it is free, so we will not need to worry about any of the added costs.

It is going to be based on the Debian system, so you will be able to use it in any manner that you would like to get your devices to behave in the proper manner.

You will quickly notice that the Raspbian operating system is going to work just in this manner.

It is also going to come with a bunch of packages, up to 35,000, in a format that makes them really easy to install on this system.

The Raspbian operating system is going to help us work on all of our projects and see improvements, and there are going to be a ton of activities when it comes to development, which means that these extensions are going to get better and better.

This is going to be an operating system that is going to have a good environment that is able to work on a desktop, so it is going to look pretty much the same as some of the other operating systems that you may spend your time on already.

Additionally, you can work with some of the menus that are out there in order to ensure that the programs that are active do the work for you here.

Using the environment that comes with Raspbian that is for the desktop is always a nice touch for those who haven't had much of a chance to work with the console that comes with Linux.

Keep in mind that this is going to be a device that has a lot of power, and it is going to lack a bit of strength in order to handle some of the bigger processes that we see with desktop computers.

This means that when it comes to doing a few activities, like 4K movies, editing videos, and photography, to name a few, it is going to be lacking a bit.

Even with some of these limitations, you will be amazed at what the Raspbian operating system is going to be able to do.

Since this operating system is going to be seen as a kind of distribution that comes with Linux, you can feel at ease knowing that your programs are going to have a few features of security, and the network capabilities are going to be higher.

We have to remember that Linux is always a good option to use for an operating system and you should be able to get a ton of projects done with the little Raspberry Pi device.

You can also choose to come in with a variety of other operating systems if you would like.

Why Should I Choose to Work with Raspberry Pi?

We have spent a good deal of time talking about the Raspberry Pi device here already, and all of the neat things that we are able to make it do along the way.

Even with this in mind, we need to take a look at some of the benefits that are going to come with using this device.

It is basically just a smaller computer that we can rely on to get our work done, and to learn some of the programming that we would like, but why is it such a great option to do all of this for us?

There are many options that a new programmer is able to choose from when they want to be able to learn a bit more about programming and what they are able to do with them.

And a lot of them are going to be able to handle the work that we need.

But a lot of them, while they are effective, are going to be a bit intimidating to someone who is a beginner and doesn't know how to handle the whole process.

The good news is that this is exactly where the Raspberry Pi is able to come in and make a difference.

Remember that Raspberry Pi is going to be a small computer that is able to handle a lot of the tasks that we want for coding and programming, and it is often doing this in a manner that is more user-friendly and easier to work with.

There are a number of benefits that come with using Raspberry Pi that include:

- The amount of power consumption.

    This device and all of the products that are in this family are not going to use up a ton of electricity in order to get all of the work done.

    You will find that this device is usually going to stay at just five to seven watts of electricity, which is about one-tenth of what a comparable full-size box is going to rely on.

    This can save a lot of money and energy in the process and can help us to get all of our tasks done in no time.

- The parts are not going to move.

    The nice thing that we will see with some of these devices is that it is going to use an SD card to help with the storage.

    This is going to be a good method to use for storage, and there are no moving parts that we need to worry about.

There are also no issues with fans or other similar parts that we need to worry about.

And it helps to improve the performance of what we work with.

- The small form factor:

The Pi, and the case you use with it, are going to be small enough that you are able to hold them in your hand.

This basically means that you are able to fit a whole computer in your hand, and it will still get things like games and other programs done.

This can make it more convenient and nice to work with.

   o The fact that this is a small device that we are able to work with is going to surprise us with all of the great things that we are able to do when it comes to technology and developing the projects that we want to work with.

   There is a ton of power that we are able to use with this board, and you will love how much you are able to do with it in no time at all.

- Limited to no noise.

When you think about your traditional kind of computer that you want to use, you may notice that there is going to be a lot of noise that comes with it.

For some of the big box computers, the noise is going to be quite loud and annoying.

But when you are working with the Pi device, you can notice that while it has a lot of power behind it, there isn't all that much noise to worry about at all.

- Status lights.

  When you bring out the Pi device and start working with the motherboard that comes with it, you will notice that there are going to be a few lights in a place that is there to tell us the status of the device.

  And when you use a clear case on the device, it is easy to see these status lights.

  These can make it easier to see whether the device is working or if there is something going on that you need to fix.

- You can easily expand out the Raspberry Pi device.

  There are a lot of different parts and devices that we are able to add to the Pi, and just like the Pi device, they are going to be affordable enough to try them out and see what you are able to do with them.

They are going to include options like a camera, a board for I/O, and more.

And the Pi is also going to come with a few ports for USB so that you are able to expand out with some other devices as you need as well or work with a powered USB hub so that you can add it with as many devices that you would like.

- A built-in graphic for HDMI.

  The display port that comes on these devices is going to be the HDMI, which means that it is able to hold onto all of the resolutions that you need up to 1920 by 1200.

  This is going to be good news because it will ensure that you can handle the imaging and videos that you need on this device.

  There are going to be some options for a few converters that you can work with that are going to help us work with the backward compatibility of our VGA.

- It is affordable.

  When you look through a lot of the other options that are available when it comes to the technology that you would like to work with, you will find that a lot of them are going to be expensive.

This can make it hard to give them a try because we can't afford them.

But when it comes to the Pi devices, you will find that it has a lot of great specs and more and an affordable price.

For example, you will find that a few of these will have up to 512 MB of RAM and will be as low as $40 to purchase.

- o Learning programming no longer needs to be as expensive as we are used to seeing.

  In a world where things cost hundreds of dollars to learn anything (buying a good computer could even cost in the thousands instead), this can be refreshing and lowers some of the objections of people who want to get into programming and making their own devices, but do not want to spend all that money.

- A lot of support in the community:

  Pi has phenomenal community support.

  This support can be obtained quite easily for the hardware and the Linux software that runs on the Pi mainly in user forums, depending on the GNU/Linux distribution used.

- o   When you are able to go through this and utilize some of the great coding languages, like Python, you can grow your community even more.

    There are a number of coding languages that we are able to use here, but Python is one of the best and easiest options out there, and the community that goes with this language can help us to learn along the way.

- Overclocking capability:

    The Pi device can be overclocked if there are some problems with the performance of the application used, but it is at the risk of the user to try and do this.

- Lots of different uses.

    You will find that since you are able to keep the storage that you need on the SD card, it makes it easy to swap with other SD cards.

    This makes it easier for you to quickly and easily change the functionality of the device—if you want to set up the Pi to run as a server to test it out—and then you can just swap out the SD card and try out something different.

And when you are done, you are able to use the "*dd*" command on your computer—you can do a backup of the SD card and keep it for restoration later if you would like.

With all of the benefits and the different positives that we are able to see with the Raspberry Pi, it is going to seem like there is nothing negative to say about it, and that everyone would be able to jump right in and enjoy it.

However, we will find a few drawbacks that come with this device, and it is important to know what those are so we can make some good and informed decisions.

The first negative that we are going to see with this is that the Pi device is going to rely on the architecture of ARM.

While this can be seen as a low powered and sometimes a highly efficient kind of architecture, it is not going to be as fast as we need in some cases.

The good news is that the GNU and the distributions that come with Linux are going to be compiled in a manner that works well with the ARM architecture, and it is possible that in the future, this is going to be something that will be changed about the Pi device so that we are able to make it work for our needs

Another issue that is going to come up with this one is that the RAM is not something that we will be able to upgrade at all.

The main components that come on the Raspberry device are soldered together on our motherboard, which is going to include the RAM at just 512 at the most.

This is not a big problem because we are still able to run the Linux and GNU that we would like, but in some cases, it may not be enough for what we want.

As we can see, there are a lot of different parts that are going to come with the Raspberry Pi device, and knowing what it is about, some of the benefits that come with the device, and more, are going to make it easier to know why so many people love it so much.

When you are ready to work with this device, and you want to be able to use it for your needs, then this is the best place to get started.

Chapter 2: Setting Up the Raspberry Pi

Now that we have some of the basics of the Raspberry Pi device down and we understand what it is about and a few of the features, it is time for us to look at a bit more at how we are actually able to use the device for our needs.

First, there are going to be a number of steps that we need to be able to take to help us ensure that this device is going to behave in the manner that we want, and will complete all of the programs that we would like along the way as well.

It takes a little bit of time for us to set up this device and to make sure that it is going to work the way that we want.

The good news is that this is not going to be as complicated as it may seem to someone who is just getting started.

There are a few steps that we need to work with, and we need to take a look at a few of the parts that come with the Raspberry Pi, and some of the accessories that we may want to consider adding in as well so that we can use this in the right manner.

In this chapter, we are going to take a look at some of the different components that we need to know in order to get started, how we can do the proper setup of the operating system how to set all the other parts up, and even how we are able to test out the program to ensure that it will work and it can do the other projects and work with programming that we want.

So, with this in mind, let's dive in!

Things to Know to Get Started in Raspberry Pi

Before we have a chance to start on this whole process, there are going to be a number of supplies that we need to go out and purchase.

These need to be on hand before we get really far in this process if we want to see it be successful.

To start, of course, we need to have the specific Raspberry Pi device that we would like.

Some of the other supplies that we are able to work with when it comes to the Raspberry Pi device include:

- A monitor or television that can take HDMI:

    You will need to be able to connect the device to some sort of display.

    A television or your computer monitor is fine as long as it can handle HDMI.

    There are also some compact options that you can choose to work with if you wish.

- A mouse and a keyboard:

    These need to be connected to a USB so that they can hook into the Raspberry Pi.

Any type will work to get this done, but they need to hook in so that you can give the device some instructions.

We can work with this without needing to have the mouse and the keyboard.

But since most people are familiar with using these on their regular computer, having these available to use on the Raspberry Pi will make it easier to get started, and can take out some of the complexities that we find with using this device.

- MicroSD card and its card reader:

  The operating system that comes with the Raspberry Pi does not use a hard drive.

  Instead, it comes with a MicroSD card already installed.

  Make sure that you get one that has at least 8GB, or you won't be able to do much with the device.

  Your personal computer might have a card reader, so if you are using that, you are probably set.

  However, if the screen you are using doesn't have this, you can find a card reader online for about $10.

- Power supply:

The Raspberry device is going to be powered through a micro USB.

This is similar to what your phone runs on.

There are four USB ports to supply power to.

Just make sure that the power supply that you choose is able to give a minimum of 2.5A of power to the device.

These are just a few of the different options that we are able to work with, and are the most basic of what we are able to use.

We are able to go through and pick out other parts based on the project that we want to handle.

Once we have all of these parts nearby and ready to use, it is time to work with the setup process to get the device to actually work.

How to Install the Operating System

To get the device to work in the manner that we would like, we need to make sure that the operating system is downloaded and ready.

Without the operating system, we are going to only end up with a device that can turn on but has a blank screen and nothing else in the process.

That is why we need to choose now the operating system that we would like to work with and go as far as actually installing this.

To work on installing the operating system that we want to work with, we first need to make sure that we have another regular computer to work with, either a desktop or a laptop.

The Raspbian operating system is going to be the one that we plan to work with, but we have first to load it onto one of our regular computers first and then use an SD card to get it transferred over to the Pi device later.

Now, you, as the programmer, will have a few choices to make here, and we are going to limit it to two.

First, it is possible to go through and make sure that the operating system for Raspbian is manually installed on the system.

This means that you have to bring in some external software to get it done, or you have to come in with enough experience in coding to get it all done by simply typing this into the command line.

Now, the second option that you can choose to work with, and the most common option that beginner programmers like to work with because it is easier is to download and install, is NOOBs.

Since this is the more favorable option for many people because it is easier, we are going to look at the main steps that are necessary to make this one happen below:

- First, we need to bring out the SD card that we would like to use for the card reader on the computer.

- Using our computer, we are going to spend a few minutes downloading the NOOBs.

    There should be a few options for us to choose from when we get to this.

    You can explore these options, but to make it easier, we will choose the option for "offline and network install."

    This is the option that will allow us to download the Raspbian operating system.

- There are some situations where we will need to do some formatting of our SD card as FAT.

  If this is the case with your card, then you are able to download this tool for formatting simply from the SD Association.

  From the website of sdcard.org, you will need to look for the part that says "Format Size Adjustment."

  Make sure that part is on in your options menu, and then your card will be all ready to go.

- This is going to be a process that will help us to end up with a good zip file to work with.

  You are then able to extract the operating system from here.

  When the extraction is done, you can make sure that you copy all of the contents of the folder to the SD card.

  When this copying process is done, take the SD card from the card reader, or the computer that you are using, and get it back into the Raspberry device.

Now we have an SD card that has the Raspbian operating system on it, and that SD card should be on the Raspberry Pi device that we want to work with.

This will ensure that we are able to do some of the work that we want with this device because we need to have that operating system in place to make all of this work.

How to Hook Up Our Raspberry Pi Device

Now that we have taken the time to work on downloading and installing our operating system, it is time for us to go through and ensure that each and every device that we are going to use with our Pi device can be hooked up and connect properly to it.

This is going to be a pretty simple step to work with because you will just have to take on all of the parts and then plug them into the USB ports that are already found on our Raspberry Pi.

However, you may find that when you use the following order, it is going to make sure that it is all done well.

The method that we will have below is going to be the best to use because it will ensure that if you hook up a device to your Pi, that the Raspberry Pi is going to be able to recognize that device when it boots up.

The most effective method of working with this device and all of the booting that you want to work with will include the following:

1. Start by connecting the monitor to the device.
2. When the monitor is recognized, you can connect the keyboard and the mouse as well.

3. If you want to work with an Ethernet cable in order to get your internet, then this is the time to connect it.

4. And finally, connect the power that you are using.

   Since this device doesn't come with a power switch, as soon as that power source gets plugged into the device, then the device will turn on.

Setting Up Raspbian

At this point, we have had a chance to go through and get the operating system over to our SD card and ready to go.

But now we need to make sure that we boot things up, especially the NOOBs that we talked about a bit earlier so that we can use our device.

This is something that takes a few minutes, so you have to be prepared that nothing is going to happen right away.

The reason for this is that the program of NOOBs is going to take a bit of time to format the SD card it is on and will do a check to make sure that the other parts are set up well.

Keep this in mind and don't get really impatient with the speed here.

Even though it is fine to get excited at this point and want to use the Raspberry Pi, you need to take your time and allow the NOOBs program some time to get all of the tasks completed that are necessary.

If you try to rush through all of this, or you work on skipping ahead on it, this will cause some corruption in the process, and your system is not going to work well.

After the NOOBs program has had a few minutes to do the tasks that are necessary, you should notice on the Pi that there is a little screen that shows up.

This screen is going to ask us to install the operating system that we would like to use on the device.

You are going to be able to pick out any of the operating systems that you want here, but we are going to continue on with the steps to do Raspbian, as we talked about earlier.

Some of the steps that we need to do to make this happen will include:

1. Look towards the bottom of your console screen.

There should be a place there where you are able to select the keyboard layout, as well as the language, based on your region.

2. Look for the Raspbian operating system and then check that box.

   This tells the system to install the operating system.

3. NOOBs will take on the work to install this operating system.

   This does take a little bit to complete, up to 20 minutes, so be patient.

   When the Raspbian operating system is uploaded, you will be taken to the desktop for Raspbian, and you can configure everything else that you need.

How to Configure the Raspberry Pi

When we get to this point, you should notice that the Raspberry Pi device is set up and ready to go.

You should be able to look on the device and see your operating system, and that there is a nice start menu for you to use in place.

However, there are still a few other steps that we need to work with so that the Raspberry Pi device is going to work well, and we can start with these at the start menu.

So, go to the start menu and click on it. You can then click on the part for applications.

Then click so that you open up the file browser.

This is where we are able to go through and enter any of the commands that you would like so that the system knows what it is supposed to do.

This is going to be a similar process to what other operating systems are going to work with, and we will look at a few of the most common commands for this as we go through this.

There are a few other options that we need to look at with setting up the Raspberry Pi device before we get to those commands as well.

We are going to look at some of these now, including how to install and do all of the setups that are needed for the Bluetooth and Wi-Fi capabilities on this device so we can work on various projects and get this to behave in the manner that we want in the long term.

Connecting the Raspberry Pi to Your Home Wi-Fi

You will be happy to notice when it comes to this device is that it is pretty easy to connect the Raspberry Pi to your home Wi-Fi.

In fact, you will be able to work with a lot of the same kinds of steps to hook up the Raspberry Pi to the internet as you would with one of your regular computers, whether it is your own laptop or a desktop computer.

If you have done that in the past, then hooking up the Raspberry Pi device is going to be easy.

To start with this, the first step is to look for the icon for networks, which should be found on the man menu of your Pi device.

Make sure to click on this one.

This is going to be a simple icon that just looks like there are two main computers that are right next to one another, and it should be somewhere on the top and to the right of your screen.

When you are able to find that icon, you are able to click on it and then search for the Wi-Fi that you would like to use for this.

Click on the chosen network, enter the username and the password, and wait for it to connect.

And that is really all there is to this process.

You have to make sure that you are using the right Wi-Fi and that you know the password and the username, but after a few moments of connecting, you will have the Raspberry Pi device as one of your network devices, and it will be ready to go.

Connecting to the Bluetooth Devices

In addition to hooking up your Raspberry Pi device to your home internet, it is time to learn how to connect the device over to Bluetooth.

There are times when you need to make this happen for a lot of the projects that we are going to focus on along the way as well.

This could be as simple as hooking up a keyboard or a mouse to the device so that you can use it more like a traditional computer, though this is not the only limit that you can place on this.

Setting this up is only going to take a few steps to accomplish.

The first step is to go to your screen on the Pi and then check where the Bluetooth icon is located.

Click on this icon, and then you can look for the option that is there to Add Device.

Click there, and then go through and search for all of the options that are presented to you there.

Find the one that you would like to pair up with your device, and then follow the directions that show up on the screen so that you can get this whole process to finish.

And that is really all there is to this whole process.

Just by going through and doing a simple search and clicking on the right icons along the way, you are able to enable Bluetooth on this device and get the Pi to work with any of the other Bluetooth enabled devices that you would like.

Once you can get these devices to sync up with one another, you are able to get them to work together, similar in the manner that you see with some of the options on your regular computer.

Connecting to Raspberry Pi Remotely

The final thing that we are going to take a look at here is how we are able to hook up to our Raspberry Pi device in a remote manner.

This is possible, and there are some situations where you may be doing some work on Raspberry Pi, and you notice that you need to get onto the device in a remote manner.

Perhaps, at the time, you are not able to get the monitor near you to hook up, or you just need to work with that device when it is not sitting right next to you.

This is something that we are able to do pretty easily when it comes to the Raspberry Pi device.

And we are able to use it just like we would with a regular computer, so the process is not too hard to understand and work with.

Some of the options that are at your disposal in order to connect remotely to the Raspberry Pi will include:

- Use the command line to connect:

    You are able to use SSH from any computer in your home.

This allows you to get ahold of the interface for command lines on the Raspberry Pi.

While this option means that you can't access a graphic interface, you would instead be able to run any command that you want through the Terminal.

When the command is sent through the Terminal, it is going to execute on the Raspberry Pi 3.

This is a useful thing to try out any time that you have a project that doesn't really need a screen to get the work done.

- Work with VNC to make another computer the remote screen:

If you need to access the Raspberry Pi remotely and you need to work with the graphical interface, then the virtual network computing, or the VNC, is the best bet.

You will then be able to see the desktop from the Raspberry device on your computer desktop and then control it as needed.

This option is kind of slow, so you shouldn't use it all the time.

But for occasional use to make things easier, it can be a great option.

When you are able to end up at this point, you will know that you have a Raspberry Pi device that has all of the setup process and the configurations that you need ready to go.

It should be all ready for you to start working with and using.

We have made sure that there is an operating system on the device that will work with the Wi-Fi and your Bluetooth if you need it, and you can even work with this remotely to get some of the things done that you would like.

With all of this setup and ready to go, it is now time to move on to the next step.

We are now going to spend some of our time learning more about the codes and the programming that you are able to do with Pi and this device so that you can actually learn from it and get it set up to do what you would like.

Chapter 3: How to Navigate Through the Raspberry Pi

The next thing that we are going to focus on here is how to work on navigating through some of the different parts that are found in the Raspberry Pi device.

In the previous chapters, we took some time to learn more about this device and what it can do, and we did all of the setup steps that are necessary to help this work.

With that behind us, it is time to learn a few of the basics of going through the files, folders, and menus that we need to use on this device.

Even on a device that is as simple to work with as the Raspberry Pi, you will find that there are a lot of files, folders, and menus to work with, and knowing how we are supposed to use them and even how we can work with them is going to make a big difference in the amount of work that we can get done with this device.

So, let's take a look at them and learn more about what they all mean.

The Important Files in Raspberry Pi

The very first thing that we need to explore and gain more understanding about when it comes to this device is the files.

If you would like to use the command line that is present in order to edit some of our files, then we need to work with the editor of Linux.

There are a few options available for these, including Nano, Vi, and Emacs, so you can shop around and see what is the best.

We are going to focus on the Nano editor to see how this can work.

It is the default editor that comes installed with Raspberry Pi, so that makes it easier.

To get this up, you can type in "*nano file.txt*," and then you will be able to edit the file that you want.

Then press on CTRL + X to exit the program or the file when you are done.

You can press the CTRL+O to save your file when you are done.

To start though, we are going to use the command below in order to access the important files:

sudo nano /etc/wpa_supplicant/wpa_suplicant.conf

This is an important file to work with because it is going to be the one that adjusts the connectivity to the Wi-Fi that our Pi device has to the internet.

We can then go through and enter in the name or the SSID (if we know it) of the network, and then the password.

Along with these new parameters that are in place, we are able to enter in a lot of options that will make it easier to find the information about the network that we want.

For example, it is possible for us to add information about whether the wireless network is one that is open or hidden, as well as other important facts.

Once we have been able to open up this particular file, you can then go through to the very end of the file, and make sure to work with the following code to help:

network = [

    ssid="The_SSID_from_earlier"

    ask="Your_wifi_password"

From this, you are able to change the default values that are there and get them to match the parameters of your network.

You will need to use the "*sudo reboot*" command in order to restart the Raspberry Pi to make this work.

You can go through and verify whether you were able to get this wireless network to hook up on your device by going to the command line and typing in "*ifconfig wlano*".

If filed "*inet addr*" has value, this means that the device was connected to the wireless successfully.

If you find that there isn't value there, then it is time to double-check the parameters of the network again.

You can use the code below to do this:

sudo nano /etc/default/keyboard

Now, one thing to notice here is that the keyboard of the Pi device may be in GB rather than the US.

This can cause some issues with the signs that you get.

If you are using some of the codes that are needed here, make sure to take the time to change the keyboard layout from the GB over to the US to ensure that you are able to get what you need.

How to Navigate the Desktop Environment Menus

When we are working with the great Raspbian operating system on this device, you will find that the idea of the menus and more are going to be pretty simple to work with.

There is going to be one of the big and main menus that is simple enough to reach because you just need to click on Raspberry, which is on the top and the left of the screen.

This main menu is going to include all of the submenus with it, such as help, accessories, preferences, games, office, programming, and the internet.

The programming menu is first on the list.

This is going to be the part that will hold onto all of the tools that are going to be useful when you want to do developing on this device.

This means that we will usually find the IDLE editor for Python there.

Then we can go to the submenu that is there for the office.

This is going to have a few of the other tools that we would like to work with, including the LibreOffice tools.

The submenu that is there for the internet, though, is going to come with a few of the different browsers that are found and accessible on your particular device.

Many people also like being able to work with some of the devices that are installable on this as well, but you do need to take some caution when working with this part.

This is because you would want to pick out games that are not only ones that you enjoy and want to play, but they can't take up a lot of space on the Raspberry Pi (remember the memory amount is limited), and they can't require a lot of special hardware.

You can find a lot of games though that have been specially formatted to work on the Pi device, so this should not be a problem.

Then it is time for us to move on to the accessories submenu that is there.

This is going to be a good place to head if you would like to find a variety of tools, like a keyboard that works onscreen, and other tools that make working on this device easier.

Then we move on to the help submenu, which is going to provide us with the information and instructions if we ever get stuck.

It will include resources, instruction manuals, and guides to help us work with this device.

The next kind of submenu that we are able to find here is going to be known as preferences.

This is going to be something that you get to mess with a little bit because as you make a few changes to the device, you can add things here so that it is going to be set up and work in the manner that you want.

This is going to be the one that will provide you all of the information that you need on the configuration of your device.

While we are in this window, keep in mind that there are a few different things that we are able to use it for.

For example, it allows you to go in and change up the name on the device, pick out the best ways to boot up the device (you can choose to do this through the desktop or the command line), you can make changes to your password, enable SSH, and do an auto-login.

These are just a few of the different options that are available for you to try and add to the preferences submenu as you work on the device some more.

As you can see here, there are actually quite a few things that you are able to do when it is time to bring out the Raspberry Pi device, and you will be able to access all of the files and other parts that you need with ease.

One of the best things that you can do when you first get the device, to ensure that it actually works in the manner that you want, and to make it easier to understand how it works and what you can do with it, is to just play around with it.

Get the operating system set up and ready to go and then turn on the device.

Take a look at each of the menus and submenus, and see what is found there.

> This will make it easier to see what is found on the device, and what you are able to do with it, which will, in turn, ensure that we are able to get the most out of the device before we even try to work with any of the projects that we want to do later on.

Chapter 4: Writing Our Own Python Programs in the IDLE

Now that we have had a chance to go through and look at some of the fun things that we are able to do with the Pi device, and had a chance to look at the basics of installing the operating system and more on our Pi device, it is time to get down to business and look at some of the great things that we are actually able to do with this device.

And in this chapter, we are going to introduce the Python programming language, learn how it works a bit, how to add it into the Pi device, and then start with some coding that will help us to really get the device to work in the manner that we want.

While there are many programmers who are going to stick with Raspbian and use this as the chosen coding language that they want to use on the Raspberry Pi, many beginners will find that working on the Python language is a lot easier.

Python is a really easy coding language to work with and is often the chosen option for those who have never spent any time learning coding at all in the past.

While there are a lot of reasons that we can enjoy the Python language, such as it being easy even for a beginner to learn how to use and how to code in no time, it is going also to be strong enough to get the programs done that we want in a short amount of time.

However, before you can go through and write out a program with the help of this language, we need to make sure that we are using the right IDLE editor on Pi so that it actually works.

That is what we are going to spend some time learning how to do in this chapter.

So, to make this happen, one of the first steps that have to happen is to download the IDLE editor for Python and then install it on our device.

The IDLE is something that we are able to easily download right from the Python website, which is "https//python.org/downloads".

The IDLE is important for actually having a good environment to write out the codes we want, and it is going to stand for the Integrated Development and Learning Environment.

There are a lot of benefits that we are able to utilize not only with the Python language but also when we actually work with the proper IDLE editor to write out the codes that we want to do in Python.

However, some of the features that we are going to notice with this particular IDLE, rather than some of the other ones that are out there for Python, includes:

1. Use the Tkinter GUI toolkit in order to code in pure Python.
2. It is able to work on many platforms.

    This IDLE is set up to work on Mac OS X, Unix, and Windows, and it is going to work and look pretty much the same.

3. It includes the Python shell window, which is the interactive interpreter, with the colorizing of error, output, and input messages in the code.
4. There is also a multi-window text editor that has a lot of features that you will find helpful when you are working on your code.

    Some of the features that you are able to use with this include auto-completion, call tips, smart indent, Python colorizing, and multiple undo.

5. You are able to search inside any window, search through more than one file, and replace things inside the editor window.

6. There is also a debugger in this IDLE that has persistent breakpoints, stepping, and viewing of both the local and the global namespaces.

7. It includes browsers, configuration, and other dialogs.

Once you are on the right page to help us download the IDLE, you can then go through and choose out which of the versions of Python you would like to work with.

Right now, we are going to pick from Python 2 or Python 3.

The differences are not much other than a few features, but most people decide that Python 3 is the best option to help them because it is the most recent version.

There are a few instances when Python 2 is going to be the best one to work with, so do a bit of research and learn which is the best for your needs.

After you have gone through and are done with the download page that we had above, and you clicked to get this over on your system, it is going to begin with a good install here.

You need to allow a few minutes to get the install done.

You can then run the IDLE by finding it on the menu for applications.

Once we have this IDLE running, keep in mind that we are then going to have two main methods to work with to write out all of the Python programs that we need in this editor.

The first one is to write out the code in our console.

The second one is to open up a document that is new, write out the whole program we want, save it, and then run the code when it is time to do so.

Both of these methods work and professionals, as well as beginners, swear by both of them.

Often the choice is going to depend more on the method that you like the best.

When we enter into the next section, we will look at both of these examples and see which one is the most likely to work for your needs so you can make the decision.

To make it simple, you will find that if your goal is to find a good way to test out a part of your code, or if you are working with a relatively small piece of code, then you want to write it out in the console to make things easier.

But if you plan to work with a long piece of code and write out a big program, then you would want to work with the document instead.

Writing Code in Your Console

So, we are going to take a look at how we can write out some of the codes that we want to use right in the console.

When we want to write out a small bit of code, then we will want to work with the console, and we have to enter it all going one row at a time.

Then, when we are done with the row, we can press on the button of Enter so that we end up on the next line.

When you work with this, and you start it out with the def keyword, the program is then going to recognize that we would like to write out a type of code that is known as a function.

Once you have entered the function, which we will show the code for in a moment, you will then need to click on the Enter button so that you can go to the next line.

After you are done with that function and the command, you can then call it up with a passing string argument.

To see how this is going to work, look at the code example that we have below

>>>def printString(text):

    print (text):

return

>>>printString("Hello World"):

Hello World

>>>

When you go through and type this into your editor, you are going to get the result of Hello World to show up on your screen.

We are going to spend some time talking about functions a bit more in the next chapter, but this is a good introduction to help you get started.

Writing Code in a New Document

Writing out some simple codes that are only a few lines long, like what we did above, is going to be just fine to work within the console.

You do not need to go through the same amount of work as we will look at in a moment just to write out a few lines of code overall.

But when we want to write out a whole program on the Raspberry Pi, then we need to make sure that we are able to handle some of the edits and more that may show up along the way, and working on it in a document that we are able to save is a better option.

When we would like to write out some of our programs in Python in a document, we will then be able to save the various parts that go with it.

It is necessary in this case to get into the IDLE editor that we already installed earlier, and then we can go to the top and the left of our screen where File is located.

Then click on New File to continue on.

When you have clicked on the two options, then you should see a new window pop up that you can work on.

From here, the first thing that we need to work on is to save the file that we want to work with.

You can either choose to click on the file and then Save or just use the command CTRL+S.

After you have been able to save the file, you can paste the code that we used in the previous example into the new file.

When the code is ready, you can run it by simply pressing the Run option, and then clicking on either F5 or Run Model.

One thing to note here is that if your file isn't saved, the program is going to prompt us to save it.

Once you decide to run the code, it is going to be executed in the Python Shell or the main window.

As you are able to see here, both of the methods for writing out your codes are going to be simple and easy to work with.

The second option though is usually going to be the best one if you want to write out long codes and programs because it is going to make it easier to save your work as you do it, and will ensure that if there is something that goes wrong with the computer or the system while you do the work, you will not lose all of that code in the process.

How to Write Python Comments

Before we end here, we need to look at another important part that is going to come with writing codes in Python, whether you are doing it on your Raspberry Pi device or in another computer system.

And this is a discussion on the comments and how they work in this language.

There are going to be some situations when you are working on your codes, whether they are simple codes or more advanced, and you will need to go through and add in a little note about a particular part of the code.

This could be a part where you will name the code, tell yourself or another person a bit more about what you planned on doing in that part of the code, or even just to leave a message of some other sort in the code.

However, even though you are leaving these little notes, you do not want them to come through and actually affect or slow down the program that you are writing out at the time.

In order to write out one of these Python comments and get them to work, without ruining the rest of your code because the editor tries to execute them, you need to use the # or hash character, and then extend it to the end of the line.

You are able to use these comments either at the beginning of the line, or you can do it at the end when the rest of the code is done for that part.

If you do this in the proper manner, you will find that you are able to write out these comments, and they are not going to make any changes to the code and the output that you get.

In fact, when you write out the codes that you would like to use, and you execute it, the comments are not even going to be seen or noticed when you run the program.

They are just there as a point of clarification, not as an important part of the code.

You do have the option to add in as many or as few of these comments as you would like based on your code.

You could have these on every line of the code if you would like.

The general rule here is that you do not want to go through and add in too many because it makes a big mess of the code and makes it harder to read through.

As we can see here, there are a lot of parts that come together when we work with the Python code.

We need to make sure that we have the IDLE editor up and running and working on our Raspberry Pi to ensure that it is going to behave n the manner that we need to write out codes.

And then, we are able to go through and actually start doing some codes in Python to create the programs that we want in the process.

Basic Patterns in Python

Now that we are at this point, it is time for us to look at a few of the things that we are able to do when we want to write out a few codes in Python.

This is a great language to work with when we are beginners in Python, and we are not sure what steps we need to take and haven't ever done any coding at all.

And that is why we are going to jump right in here and learn a bit more about how to do some of the coding that we need in this language.

The first thing that we are going to explore here is some of the basic patterns that are important when it comes to working with Python.

One thing that you will notice about the regular expressions that we will talk about in a bit is that you will not just be stuck working on a specific fixed character to make these work.

They can also be there to make sure that you are actively looking for the patterns that are needed.

Some of the most common of the regular expressions that we are able to work with here include:

1. a, X, 9, <—Ordinary characters just match themselves exactly.

The meta-characters that aren't going to match themselves simply because they have a special meaning include: ^ $ *? { [ ] and more.

2. . (the period)—This is going to match any single except the new line symbol of "\n."

3. \w—This is the lowercase w that is going to match the "word" character.

    This can be a letter, a digit, or an underscore.

    Keep in mind that this is the mnemonic and that it is going to match a single word character rather than the whole word.

4. \b—This is the boundary between a non-word and a word.

5. \s—This is going to match a single white space character, including the form, tab, return, newline, and even space.

    If you do \S, you are talking about any character that is not a white space.

6. ^ = start, $ = end—These are going to match to the end or the start of your string.

7. \t, \n, \r—These are going to stand for the tab, newline, and return.

8. \d—This is the decimal digit for all numbers between 0 and 9.

   Some of the older regex utilities will not support this, so be careful when using them.

9. \—This is going to inhibit how special the character is.

   If you use this if you are uncertain about whether the character has some special meaning or not to ensure that it is treated just like another character.

These are just a few of the different expressions that are considered regular that work in the Python language and can show up in our code.

These are going to be important patterns that we are able to work with and learn about in this language, so we need to practice with them a bit on the IDLE editor that we already installed and get some practice with them.

Handling Our Regular Expressions

We talked about regular expressions a bit already here, but now we need to bring them more to light and see what they are all about.

Any code that you want to write in Python will need to focus at least a little bit on these regular expressions.

And the first place we are able to look at when it comes to these is the standard library that comes with Python.

You will often add in these regular expressions to help with your coding when you want to be able to look at texts and then filter them out.

It is also possible that we are going to use them to write out some codes and then check whether or not a string or a specific part of the text is going to be found in that code, and then to see whether it is actually able to match up with the regular expression that we are using here or not.

Once you can get this done in coding in Python, it is going to be a simple process, and you can even translate this into some of the other coding languages that you may want to use later.

Thus, what are regular expressions, and how are you going to learn how to make them work inside of the codes that you want to write?

A good place to start when it comes to regular expressions is to bring out your text editor and then find if there is a word that has been spelled in two different ways in the code.

We are going to help you do a few things with the use of regular expressions so that this problem of misspellings won't cause as big of a problem as they could.

A Look at the Loops

Another part of this process that we need to take a look at here is the loops that are found in Python.

These are going to be important, and sometimes they are compared to the conditional statements that are going to show up in this language and more, but there are some differences.

When you work with these loops, you are going to clean your current code quite a bit, and you will even be able to get a really large amount of code written, in just a few lines, without having to write out hundreds of potential lines of code.

To start with, the loops are going to be there and really useful for a programmer who will want to write out a code for any program that has to repeat something a certain number of times, or at least repeat itself until the conditions you set in them are met, and you do not want to waste that much time writing the same lines over and over again.

For example, if you are working with a code that needs a multiplication table that goes from one to ten, you really don't want to spend a lot of time writing out all of those lines over and over again.

We are able to use the idea of the loops to handle this so that we can get it done in just a few lines of code as well.

This may sound like a lot of work to focus on, but in reality, it is pretty simple to work with.

And you will be able to get many lines of code written in just a few lines once you master this art of doing it all.

The loop allows the program just to keep reading through the same part of the code over and over again until a new condition that you inserted has been met.

You have to add this condition into the code, or you will freeze up the computer because it will just go in a continuous loop over again.

There are a few types of loops that you can work with.

And the one that you choose is going to depend on what you are trying to do with the code.

Each of them is going to work depending on the thing that you are trying to get done inside the code.

The three loops that we are going to take a look at are the while loop, the for loop, and the nested loop.

The first kind of loop that we are going to take a look at in our coding here is known as the while loop.

This kind of loop is going to be the one that we are able to use when we want to make sure that our code will actually cycle through the iterations a predetermined number of times.

You are able to determine how many times these iterations occur when you write out this kind of loop to ensure that it works the way that you want.

With this kind of loop, the goal is not to get the lines of code to get stuck in the cycle an indefinite number of times.

Your goal is to make sure that it is going to go through for the exact number of times that you would like.

If you are going through a code that you want to have count from one to ten, then you want to set up this loop to go through the iteration ten times.

With this specific loop option, the loop is going to head through things a minimum of one time, and then will check to see whether the conditions have been met or not.

In the example of counting from one to ten, the loop will put up the number one, and then check to see if the conditions are checked, put up the number two, and continue on in this pattern until it gets to ten and sees that the condition is no longer met afterward.

Writing out these kinds of loops is easier than it may seem.

To help us understand how to make this work for our needs, let's take a look at some of the sample codes to see what we can do to create one of these while loops in our own codes:

```
counter = 1
while(counter <= 3):
    principal = int(input("Enter the principal amount:"))
    numberofyears = int(input("Enter the number of years:"))
    rateofinterest = float(input("Enter the rate of interest:"))
    simpleinterest = principal * numberofyears * rateofinterest/100
    print("Simple interest = %.2f" %simpleinterest)
    #increase the counter by 1
    counter = counter + 1
    print("You have calculated simple interest for 3 time!")
```

Now that we have had a chance to take a look at this kind of loop and to see what it is going to do for us, it is time to open up the compiler and practice writing the code out.

You can then execute the code and see what information will show up on the screen.

You should notice that when you are done with writing this one out, you will have the output set up so that the user is able to add in the information that they want, and then the program will do the necessary computations to figure out the interest rates, the final amounts, and so on based on the numbers that the user is able to add into this system.

As the programmer, you get to go through and determine how many loops you would like to do here, or how many times you would like the user to be able to add in numbers.

We went through this one so that the loop progressed three times, but you do have the freedom to add in more or less depending on your goals with the program.

The second option that we are able to work with is a for loop.

There is enough power and strength that comes with the while loop that we are able to use that for most of our loop needs in Python; there are a few times when we need to work with a loop that is slightly different than the while loop.

This is going to bring us to the for loop.

The for loop is usable in a lot of different situations, and it is actually seen as the more traditional method of writing and creating the loops that we want to use.

When it is time to bring out the for loop, it is time for us to set it up in a manner that the user isn't the one who comes in and provides the information to this program. Instead, you will decide when the loop is supposed to stop instead.

This is going to make it easier for the loop to go through the iteration, going through it in the exact order that we add them to the loop.

This information is then going to show up on your computer screen, and the user will not need to go through the process of inputting anything in the meanwhile.

A good example of the code that we are able to work with here includes:

Measure some strings:

words = ['apple,' 'mango,' 'banana,' 'orange']

for w in words:

print(w, len(w))

When you work with the for loop example that is above, you are able to add it to your compiler and see what happens when it gets executed.

When you do this, the four fruits that come out on your screen will show up in the exact order that you have them written out.

If you would like to have them show up in a different order, you can do that, but then you need to go back to your code and rewrite them in the right order, or your chosen order.

Once you have then written out in the syntax and they are ready to be executed in the code, you can't make any changes to them.

And then, we are ready to move on to the third type of loop.

This nested loop is going to take some of the other loops that we talked about to the next level.

But this opens up a lot of the different parts that we want to work with and can add in some more complexities along the way.

With the nested loop, we are working with the process of taking one loop and then making sure that it is placed inside of another loop.

You will find that both of these loops will then be able to keep going over and over until both of them have had a chance to reach their completion along the way.

This is going to seem a little bit strange when we work on them in some of our code.

Why would you really want to go through the process of working with two loops and having them run together at the same time?

But there are actually a ton of programs that you are able to do with this, and learning how to create your own nested loops is important.

For example, if you are working with a code that needs to have a multiplication table inside of it.

Rather than writing out hundreds of lines to make this one happen, which is what it would take if you did this in any other manner, you would just need to do a few lines in order to make this happen.

And it is easier to work with than it seems.

Writing out this code is simple enough to handle. Some of the codes that we are able to utilize here include:

#write a multiplication table from 1 to 10

For x in xrange(1, 11):

    For y in xrange(1, 11):

    Print '%d = %d' % (x, y, x*x)

When you got the output of this program, it is going to look similar to this:

1*1 = 1

1*2 = 2

1*3 = 3

1*4 = 4

All the way up to 1*10 = 2

Then, it would move on to do the table by twos such as this:

2*1 = 2

2*2 = 4

And so on until you end up with 10*10 = 100 as your final spot in the sequence.

Go ahead and put this into the compiler and see what happens.

You will simply have four lines of code, and end up with a whole multiplication table that shows up on your program.

Think of how many lines of code you would have to write out to get this table the traditional way that you did before?

This table only took a few lines to accomplish, which shows how powerful and great the nested loop can be.

Handling Your Inheritances

Another topic that we need to take a look at when we are trying to write out some of our own codes in Python is the idea of an inheritance.

We have talked about a lot of options, but we will enjoy the fact that Python is an OOP language and can work with something like an inheritance.

With the inheritance, we will be able to work with a process of creating our own parent class, and then we will use it through the code over and over again, turning it into a child class and making the necessary changes and additions to that second code to help keep our code organized and easy to work with.

When you bring out the inheritance in your code, this means that you are just going to take some of your original code, which is known as the parent or the base code, and then you can copy it down further on inside of the code, and that new one will be known as the child code or the derived code.

The child code that we just worked on will start out being the same as the parent code when you begin with it.

But we are able to take this a bit further as well.

The programmer is able to take that child code that they have and make the adjustments and other changes that you would like.

This helps the child code work in the manner that we would like, without having to worry about messing with the parent class or how it functions in the first place.

One of the nice parts of working with the child code is that you can make as many changes and adjustments as we would like.

This is going to allow you a way to make the adjustments that you would like, and any of the changes necessary, without having to worry about the way that it will affect the parent code that you borrowed it from.

And then there is the benefit of just working with one of the legs of the inheritances, or you are able to go through and make a line of these child codes as well.

This may sound like it is complex to work with when you are ready to handle your Python codes, but it is going to be a simple code to help us learn some of the power that comes with Python.

You can then make the changes that you want along the way.

Let's take a look at some of the coding that we are able to use to create and work with our own inheritances includes:

```python
#Example of inheritance
#base class
class Student(object):
    def __init__(self, name, rollno):
        self.name = name
        self.rollno = rollno
#Graduate class inherits or derived from Student class
class GraduateStudent(Student):
    def __init__(self, name, rollno, graduate):
        Student __init__(self, name, rollno)
        self.graduate = graduate
def DisplayGraduateStudent(self):
        print("Student Name:", self.name)
        print("Student Rollno:", self.rollno)
        print("Study Group:", self.graduate)
#Post Graduate class inherits from Student class
class PostGraduate(Student):
    def __init__(self, name, rollno, postgrad):
```

Student__init__(self, name, rollno)

self.postgrad = postgrad

def DisplayPostGraduateStudent(self):

print("Student Name:", self.name)

print("Student Rollno:", self.rollno)

print("Study Group:", self.postgrad)

#instantiate from Graduate and PostGraduate classes

objGradStudent = GraduateStudent("Mainu", 1, "MS-Mathematics")

objPostGradStudent = PostGraduate("Shainu", 2, "MS-CS")

objPostGradStudent.DisplayPostGraduateStudent()

When you type this into your interpreter, you are going to get the results:

('Student Name:,' 'Mainu')

('Student Rollno:', 1)

('Student Group:', 'MSC-Mathematics')

('Student Name:', 'Shainu')

('Student Rollno:', 2)

('Student Group:', 'MSC-CS')

As you can see, there are a lot of different parts that we are able to work with when it comes to handling our own codes in the Python language, learning how to work with some of this, and ensuring that we are able to write out some of our own codes and use this for some of our programs when it comes to using the Raspberry Pi device.

Chapter 5: How to Use the Raspberry PI

Now that we are done working with some of the coding that we are able to do when we work on the Raspberry Pi device, it is time for us to go a bit further and learn how to work with this Raspberry Pi along the way.

Setting up the Pi to make sure that it works with the sensors, diodes, and other things that you want can sometimes be a challenge.

However, we are going to spend some of our time talking about how we can handle this to make sure that we get the full use out of Raspberry Pi.

How to Interface Our Electronics

You will find that the Raspberry Pi device is pretty much useless if you have not been able to figure out how to interact and use the device at all.

Here, we are going to spend our time looking at the best way to get the Pi set up, and make sure that the electronics that you want to use.

This section will help us to learn some more about how to set up the Pi so that it is able to work well, whether you want to use it on its own, or you want to use this with some other electronics.

The first option that we need to work with here is making sure that we have the proper equipment in order to make sure that you are able to get this to work, and then destroy your circuit or even your Raspberry Pi.

One of the tools that we need to work with here is the multimeter.

It is best to work with one that is digital.

It is important that you have one before any of the other work with the circuitry is done with this device.

Keep in mind that the Raspberry Pi device is going to be able to help us out with measuring out a lot of different things, including the voltage, current, and resistance.

This is going to ensure that you won't start to pump on the circuit and give the device more than it is able to handle.

In addition to the multimeter, though, we need to make sure that we have a few other components in place to help us get started.

Some of these will include:

　　1.　Diodes:

This is going to be a semiconductor component that simply allows one current to flow in one direction and ensures that this current is not allowed to flow in the other direction.

2. Light-emitting diodes or LEDs:

    This LED is going to act in a similar manner as a diode, just that it emits light of some color if the current flows in the right direction.

    There are many colors, sizes, and shapes for you to choose from with the LEDs.

    The length of the leg is going to determine which of the legs is positive and which one is negative.

3. Capacitors:

    A capacitor is going to be a component that can be used in order to store some of the electrical energy that you need.

    This can be useful when you want to store energy when there is a big difference in voltage between the two plates.

    Once the difference in voltage is able to dissipate, it is going to help to release the energy that is stored to ensure that it doesn't harm the Pi device.

4. Transistors:

A transistor is going to be a semiconductor component that can be used to amplify or switch electricity or electric signals.

5. Optocouplers:

These are helpful because they are going to be digital switching devices that ensure that you are able to isolate two electrical circuits from one another.

6. Switches and buttons:

These are going to be pretty self-explanatory.

These are going to be the input devices that you interact with to make sure that the circuit does something.

Their basic function is to open or close a circuit.

They will come in different shapes and forms, depending on what you would like to do with them.

Understanding Communication Protocols

The next thing that we want to spend our time here is some of the communication protocols that are out there.

To make sure that the system that we have is going to work well, and that there is some good communication going on between the components, we need to make sure that we are taking care of the right protocols to make this happen.

There are already a few standards that we are able to look for, and ones that are already in place and that we need to follow, that are there to make sure that the communication between the Raspberry Pi and other devices is going always to be consistent and coherent.

These will be known as our communication protocols.

As we go through this, you will quickly notice that there are going to be a few different types of communication protocols that we can work with here.

And the difference between them is going to make it easier for us to understand how we work with the different concepts as well.

Some of the most important concepts that we are able to work with when it comes to these communication protocols include:

1. Bitrate:

   This is going to be the part that helps us to describe how many bits are sent per unit of time.

2. Band rate:

   While we are going to see the bit rate is able to describe the number of bits that we have, the band rate is going to help us to describe how many symbols are going to be sent per unit of time that we want to use.

   The symbols can each come in as any number of bits that we want, and it often depends on the design that we work with.

3. Parallel communication:

   When we work with this one, the bits are going to be sent out so that just one goes out at the same time.

4. Serial communication:

   This is going to be a type of communication where the bits will be sent out just one at a time.

5. Synchronous serial communication:

   This is going to be the protocol that we are able to use for serial communication where all of the data that we are going to use will be sent out in a stream that is continuous and steady.

This is going to require that the internal clocks of the systems that we embed will be synchronized at the same rate to help the receiver get all of the signals at regular intervals.

6. Asynchronous serial communication:

   When we are working with this one, we will find that this will not require us to have an internal clock that is synchronized.

   This data stream is going to contain some of the start and the stop signals that happen before and after the transmission, respectively.

   When we get it so that the receiver starts with the right start signal, it is going to then prepare them for the incoming data stream.

   But when the signal to stop comes in, it is going to reset itself so that it can be open to a new stream coming in at a later time.

Doing Some Real-Time Interfacing with Arduino

If you are not that familiar with how to work on this, you will find that the microcontroller of Arduino can be something that is powerful to work with.

You will be able to use it, along with the Raspberry Pi, to help us work on some of the best projects.

Of course, to make all of this work, you have to also have an Arduino board.

You will also need to go through a good amount of expertise and mastery of programming in interfacing to make this all work.

Of course, this is going to take some more time than we have for it in this guidebook, so it is important to do some of your own research on the topic if you would like to do that.

Though we won't spend that much time in this guidebook working with this kind of interfacing, you will find that there are a few key things that you need to keep in mind for this including:

1. It is possible to do some interfacing with the Arduino board if you would like to use any of the other protocols of communication like the ones that we talked about before.
2. It is also able for us to configure the Arduino as an IC slave. This means that you will be able to connect back to

more than one of the Arduino boards to help out if you would like.

3. You will be able to use a connection that is straightforward UART.

    This is going to be able to support one of these options at a time so that you can get a different connection to get what you want to be done.

4. If you are looking to have a higher-level interaction and fast between the Pi device and the Arduino, then you will want to spend a bit of time configuring your board as the SPI slave is the best way for us to go.

    This is going to be due to the fact that this connection is only going to have limitations for the clock speed of the Arduino.

How to Capture Videos, and Images

It is also possible for us to work with the device of Raspberry Pi in order to get audio, record the videos, and capture all of the photos that you would like.

Of course, we do need to add in a few peripherals if you would like to get any of these actions done.

For example, you can choose to work with the USB webcam, Raspberry Pi camera, USB audio, and the audio HAT.

The first option that we are able to work with is how to use the Raspberry Pi for images and videos.

There are many options when we set this up, such as using the device to help out with home security, robotics, automation, and image or video streaming.

If you have the right extras to work with it, it is even possible for us to work with videos that are high in quality as well. This stream, when it is done using the device, you will be able to view it asynchronously.

The only limit that we are going to see here will be the duration because if you are short on storage, you are not going to be able to tape a very long video.

To get started with this, though, we need to take the time to add a camera to your device.

You can go through and either use a USB webcam, or you can go through and purchase a camera that has been built in order to work specifically with your Pi device.

We are going to work with the option for the Raspberry Pi Camera to help make this quick and not waste time with the explanation here, but you will find that the work that comes with adding on some of the other options of cameras will be similar.

To help us get started with this process, we need to make sure that we are able to get the camera of our choice attached to the Pi device.

There are going to be a few different options that we are able to use with this one including:

1. Turn the device off.

   Make sure that you don't touch the metal contacts of your ribbon cable, or you might ruin it.

2. Take the lens protector off.

3. Get the CSI connector and then gently pull up the housing clip.

   This is going to be either white or black.

4. Insert the CSI cable into its slot.

5. Now you can push down the housing clip in order to let it get locked in place.

6. Now that this is in place, you can turn the Pi device pack on and configure the camera.

   You will be able to enable the camera with the following command:

   pi@erpi ~ $ sudo raspi-config

7. Reboot the device.

If you would like to go through and capture images, you would need to input the following command:

pi@erpi ~ $ raspistill -o image.jpg

pi@erpi ~ $ ls -l image.jpg

Of course, this is just the start of what we are going to do when it is time to set up this system and make sure that it is running in the right manner as well.

It is also possible for us to go through and set up our own security system for the home or even stream some videos with this feature as well if we would like.

There are a lot of great things that we are able to do with the camera and the webcam being on the Pi device, but there are a few more steps that we will need to discuss later on in order to get all of this set up to work.

How to Record and Play Audio

For the most part, when you are doing the necessary work to take the videos that you would like, you have to make sure that there is some noise or audio that comes with it to make them actually work.

And then there are times when maybe you would like to just add in the audio that you want to use.

Sometimes, you will want to add in a speaker, for example, to help the Pi device play music or use other noises along the way.

And we are going to now look at the steps that we can take in order to make sure we can do this audio work.

So, to make sure that we are able to get the audio set up and ready to go, we have to make sure that we are getting the audio input or output device ready to go.

The cool thing to work with here is that the Pi device is going to come with its own built-in audio output system in most of the versions, and then these are going to connect right to the device with the help of the port of the HDMI.

For input, though, we need to work with an additional device to make this happen.

Some of the options that we are able to use to make this happens to include:

1. The USB audio:

    For this project to work, we need to be able to attach an input device with USB audio.

    This can be done as long as you pick out one that is able to work with some of the drivers of Linux.

    You may also work with some of the webcams of USB that we talked about before.

    We just have to go with one that comes with a microphone to make it work

2. Bluetooth Audio:

    The next thing that we are able to use here is either the audio input that works directly with Bluetooth, or you need to go with an output system in order to help connect back to the Pi device.

    We just need to make sure, like with the above, that we are choosing one that will be compatible with the Linux system for the best results.

3. Raspberry Pi HATs:

    These are going to be known as the shorthand for Hardware Attached on Top.

You are able to choose to attach one of these in order to use the various capabilities of audio that are going to be available with the Pi device.

If you would like to go through and ensure that the recording you do will have audio and work well, then you have to go through and ensure the ALSA utility software is found on your device.

This is a good software to have because it will have the play and the record utilities that are necessary for us to get all of the audio that we need.

To help us out if we still need to install this software on our own device, we can use the coding below:

pi@erpi ~ $ sudo apt update

pi@erpi ~ $ sudo apt install alsa-utils

And this should be enough to get it downloaded.

You may need to go through and reboot the Pi device to make sure that it gets on the program the way that you would like.

Now, we need to take a quick look at how you can use this software, and the tools that come with it, in order to record and play the audio that you need with either your own movies or with your music.

To record the audio, you just need to use the following command:

```
pi@erpi ~/tmp $ arecord -f ed -D plughw:1,0 -d 10 test.wav
```

And then, when you are ready to make sure that the audio is going to play, you just need to work with the following command:

```
pi@erpi ~ /tmp # aplay -D plughw:1,0 test.wav
```

As we are able to see here, there are a ton of options that we are able to focus on when we bring in the Raspberry Pi device, and we are ready to make it work for our needs.

There are so many projects and more that we are able to do with this controller, and as long as we are set up and ready to go with it, we are likely to get the results that we want in no time.

Chapter 6: Learning About the GPIO Pins on This Device

While we are spending some time on the Raspberry Pi device and all of the neat things that we are able to do with it, it is time for us to take a little detour and look a little at the pins that come with this device.

There are a number of pins that come with your board, and the amount that you are going to deal with really depends on your particular board and which one you decided to purchase in the first place.

Some boards have more pins, and some have fewer.

No matter which board we decide to go with, there are going to be several pins that are the same.

These may be a bit hard to learn about if you have never done programming in the past, but being able to work with the pins and understanding what they are used for and why each one is important is going to make a world of difference in what we are able to do with these boards overall.

In this chapter in particular, we are going to take a look at the GPIO pins.

These are the ones that are found on all of the Raspberry Pi boards that we want to work with, and can really help us to get some great results with it in no time when we want to use this device to actually create some of our own projects.

With this in mind, let's dive into some of the things that we need to know when it comes to using the GPIO pins in our own boards.

When we bring out our Raspberry Pi board and take a look at it, you have to come in with some method to use it, while also getting it to interact with the outside world.

This ability is possible, thanks to some of the GPIO pins that are found on this device.

Since these are really important to the functioning of this device, there are a ton of improvements that we can notice with these pins when we compare earlier versions of the Raspberry Pi to some of the current options.

In fact, you will find that the latest version of this device, the Raspberry Pi 3, has 40 of these specific GPIO pins found inside.

A good way for us to take a look at these pins is that they are basically going to be switched on the board, and each of them will have two states to work with.

These two states are easy to remember because they will either be the input, or they will be the output.

If we want to be able to read the data from some of the sensors, such as using a computer to tell us what temperature it is outside, then we would find ourselves in the state of the input to do this.

However, if we want to use this device to hook up some LED lights for the project, and get them to turn on and off, then we are switching over to using the output pins.

When we are talking about some of these GPIO pins on our device, there are four main colors there that can help us to know which of the different types of pins that we are dealing with at a time.

The first type of pin will be in red, and these will represent the power that we can give to our device.

Usually, the strength of these will fall somewhere between 3.3V and 5V, and it will depend on which device you are working with.

The next type of pin that we can deal with is the black pins.

These are going to be our grounds and will be the output, but instead of showing us some kind of light or another action, they are going to act more like a negative terminal of a battery so we can move the electricity around some more and get it to behave in the manner that we want.

The third type of pin that we are able to work with is the yellow pins.

These are important pins to work with because they will be the ones that we can program.

Remember that we mentioned a bit earlier that there are two states that we are able to work with on these pins, the output, and the input.

When we are handling some of the work with the output, then we are going to have our pins do a HIGH (1) or a LOW (0) setting to it, depending on whether it should have some power with it or not.

It is a bit different when we work with the input.

With this one, depending on the state of our output, we are going to see a 0 or 1, and the sensors are going to be the ones that we are going to look to when we want to figure this out.

And finally, we will end with some of the orange pins.

These are nice pins to work with because they will help us to connect some of our additional boards along to the original one that we are working with right now.

Whether you want to do this or not is going to depend on the kind of project that you are taking on.

With this in mind, we need to be able to take a look at an example of how all of this is able to work.

Let's say that we are going through, and we want to use our Raspberry Pi device to help us have some control over how a LED light is able to work.

To make this one happen, we would need to perform some of the following steps:

1. First, we have to take the shorter wire that is found with our LED light and connect it over to the proper resistor on the board.

2. When this is done, we are going to take the other side that comes with our LED light and connect it to the resistor of our GND pin on our Raspberry Pi board.

3. The final step here is that we want to take the long wire that has been connected with the LED light and make sure that it is connected to one of the yellow pins (you can choose which one you want to work with here), on the board as well.

And that is all that we would need to do in order to hook up the LED light to our board.

There would need to be a little bit of coding along here to get the setup to finish and make sure that the light would turn on or off.

But the pins that are found on our device will make it easier to hook up any of the extra components that we want, whether they are LED lights or something else, and get the work done.

It will only take a few times working through this project before we can understand how the pins work and what we are able to do with them.

Chapter 7: Easy Ways to Troubleshoot the Raspberry Pi

The final thing that we need to take a look at here when it comes to handling our Raspberry Pi device is how to do some of the troubleshooting that will make this device work in the manner that we want.

There are a lot of options that we are able to explore when it is time to open up that device and get it set up to do the work we want, but then there are also times when the device is not going to work in the manner that we want.

We need to be able to take control over this and ensure that we have the right tools that will help us to do the proper troubleshooting and get this taken care of.

This chapter is going to help us take a closer look at a number of the issues that are going to come up when we focus on the Raspberry Pi.

The main thing to remember with this one is that the Raspberry Pi is often going to work just fine, and if there is an issue, it is as simple as changing up the pins you are using or making sure that the code you wrote is actually the right one for what you are doing.

This is going to help us know that the board will be just fine, and there are plenty of options that we can try out in order to get this board to work if we do run into some trouble.

The good news when we talk about troubleshooting the Raspberry Pi is that most of the issues are common, and you can fix them on your own rather than having to seek out a professional or give up on your board.

You may find that some of the issues are as easy to fix as just resetting the device, others may be replacing some of the parts you are working with, and others could be just starting over from scratch and seeing what you may have done wrong in the process.

However, many times when our Raspberry Pi device is not working the way that we want, you will find that the issue is going to be pretty small and can be worked out quickly.

We are going to take a look here at some of the most common issues that are out there when it comes to the Raspberry Pi, and what we are able to do to try and get them fixed so that you can actually use your board and get some of the coding to work well for you.

How to Avoid a Corrupted SD Card

The first issue that we need to take a look at and one of the most common problems that show up when we work with this kind of device is that we pick out an SD card to work with that ends up being corrupted.

This isn't a very common issue, and as long as you get a good quality card to work with and don't mess with it too much, it will work with your Raspberry Pi well.

This is usually a problem that is going to show up when the SD card is a bit older because these are not going to be able to handle some of the work that you want to do with them.

If you are getting started with the Raspberry Pi device for the first time, it may be a good idea to go and get an SD card that is brand new.

This will be much better than pulling out one of the cards that are older and not able to handle some of the work as easily.

A highly rated one is a good option, such as an SDHC, and make sure that it is able to hold at least 2 GB or more.

The Pi device is going to be able to rely on storage in a manner that is similar to most high-end tablets.

This means that you have to make sure that the SD card is strong enough and has enough storage in order to get this all done.

Keep in mind here, though, that no matter which of the many SD cards that are out there that you can choose from, there are other methods that can sneak up and will corrupt our data here as well.

The first issue that can come up is if you try to remove the SD card before turning the Raspberry Pi device off. Just like with using USB storage on a Windows computer or with some other operating systems, you will find that there are rules for safely removing the SD card and other storage options from your Raspberry Pi.

In this case, it is only going to be safe to remove your SD card when the device has had time to shut down all the way.

Another issue that can be caused by your SD card is when you try to turn your Pi device off in the wrong manner.

To ensure that you are shutting down this device in a manner that is considered safe and effective, and to make sure that you do not end up with issues like a corrupt card or other problems in the process, it is important to do a bit of coding.

The coding that we are able to use to prevent this issue is "sudo shutdown -lt now".

How to Avoid Relying on Only the Main Power

And now it is time for us to move on to the second issue that we are able to do with this one.

The fact that this particular device is going to rely on the USB mains adaptor for its power is going to lead us to feel like we are secure and safe when we are using it all of the time, especially when it is time to send some of the power that we need for our projects over to the device.

This is a false sense of security.

We assume that this is safe because the USB ports are going to be similar to what we are going to find on our traditional computers and PC's, and are even found on some of the desktop monitors that we use.

This leads us to believe that we can use this connector on our Raspberry Pi device in order to get the power that we need for this small computer.

This is not a good idea to have because we need to realize that the process of powering our Raspberry Pi device is not going to be this simple.

It is possible that our device is able to receive enough power when we work with the USB 2.0 port to boot it up and then run it, running tasks that rely on a lot of processing power, or powering a USB network connection, USB storage, a mouse, and a keyboard (which are highly likely to all need to be used at the same time when you work on your projects), will often end up being too powerful for this source.

If you are using this to help power up the Raspberry Pi device and you notice that it starts to shut itself down right after you go through the booting process, then a good thing to look for here is that the small computer is not getting the amount of power that it needs and you need to change it up to something else instead.

It is usually best to not rely on this kind of power source, though because it is likely that it will not be enough for your needs.

The number one step that you can use when this is your issue is to only power the device when you actually have the proper power adapter to get the work done.

There are a number of options that are available for us to use here, and we simply need to take the time to pick out the one that is going to work on our preferences when we use the device.

Checking the Cables You Use

The third option or issue that we need to take a look at is checking out the cables that we are working with.

Keeping an eye on all of our cablings is going to be important all of the time, but it becomes even more important when we plan to use some of the custom cases that we can use with this device.

There are times when manufacturing problems can show up with the casing and the cabling of the whole thing, and when this does show up, they are going to lead us to work with power settings that are not right.

It is also possible through all of this that the Ethernet cables and the HDMI cables are going to cause us some problems as well.

In a similar manner, we need to have some awareness that sometimes the adapters that we want to work with are not made out of the high-quality options and materials that they should be.

And when this happens, they are not going to be able to keep up with some of the demand for power that you are hoping for in the process.

This is why we need to take some precautions when it comes to working with and purchasing cables to use in our projects.

Yes, it is nice to save money and get some of the cablings that does not cost as much when we do our projects, but it can have a negative effect on the projects that we are working with and may end up shorting out or having other problems.

We can look at an example of how this is able to work.

For example, the HDMI and the VGA cables and adapters can claim that they are usable, and the seller may have written out some big promises about the same thing, but faults can still arise with these.

And when these do show up, it is going to put the HDTV or the monitor of your device, as well as the device itself, at a great deal of risk when you use those cables.

This is why it is best that you take care of the extra adapters and parts that you choose to purchase for your projects.

You want to double-check and make sure that the ones you pick out are actually going to work and can provide us with the power that we really need to do well, without causing any damage or risk to the Pi device that we are using, or any of the other components that are hooked up to it as well.

And there is another thing that we need to spend a bit of time on when it comes to using our Raspberry Pi device, and this is the USB cable.

These cables are going to be designed so that they can help us out with a lot of things.

However, just because a USB cable has been designed to work well with charging up your smartphone or another similar device does not mean that it is going to be suitable to help you power up the Raspberry Pi.

This is true whether or not you went through and connected the mains adapter to the right spot.

Basically, there are a number of issues, and potential damage that could come up if you are not careful and choose out the wrong adapters for your projects, and when you are not careful about the cables that are used on this device.

This may seem like such a simple thing to work with, but we have to double-check that we are going with products that are higher in quality and can protect our device rather than going with the options that are cheaper and will end up causing a lot of harm.

If you are working with one of these Raspberry Pi devices, it is important that you are certain that, as with most of the different traditional or desktop computers you choose to work with, that you connect all of the different parts in the right manner.

Before we even take a chance at booting up our device for the very first time, we have to go through and check and confirm that we have the right cables, the right peripherals, and the necessary storage media to make this work.

Once all of those are in place properly, then you can get to work finishing up the rest of the process.

For the most part, the steps that we just talked about are going to be enough to ensure that any time your Raspberry Pi device stops working how it should, you will be able to get it fixed and up and running in no time—and when you follow these steps and are careful about the way that you treat your device, you can save a lot of time and money when it comes to dealing with data corruption or re-imaging your SD card.

Chapter 8: Simple Projects to Work within Raspberry Pi

This guidebook has taken some time to explore a lot of the neat things that we are able to do when it comes to using the Raspberry Pi device.

It is a simple board that helps us to learn more about programming and all of the neat things that we are able to do with it along the way.

With some of that behind us, though, it is time to dive right in and look at a few of the projects that we are able to create with this board.

There are a lot of projects that are possible when we work with the Raspberry Pi.

In fact, this is a device that was designed to help beginners work through some of the tough starting steps of programming and coding, so lots of projects were a must.

Some of the different projects that we are able to explore when it comes to working with the Raspberry Pi device includes:

The Arcade Box

The first kind of project that we want to take a look at is how we are able to take the Raspberry Pi device and turn it into our own little arcade box so we can play games and more.

This will give us a little bit of practice with what we are able to do with this device, and you will find that the Raspberry Pi is a good controller to use to make an arcade box because it has the potential to hold onto a lot of games, especially if you utilize various SD cards, and it is going to be easy to design into this kind of box.

Before we do that, though, there are a number of steps that the programmer has to accomplish in order to make this all happen.

We need to also make sure that we have all of the necessary tools and accessories in place to really make our own arcade box.

Some of the different supplies and options that we need to keep around when creating our own arcade box will include:

- A game controller is not necessary, but it can make playing some of the games a little bit easier.
- A power supply so that the device turns on
- The Raspberry Pi 3 (or other Raspberry Pi device that you want to use)

- A good SD card (This card needs to be at least 4GB in order to make the games work)
- An HDMI cable to hook your device up to a monitor
- A TV

The first step is to get the games from the RetroPie website over to your PI.

We are going with the RetroPie website to help us get some of the older games that we are going to use for this device.

You will simply need to download the website over to your SD card so that it can then be put on the Pi device.

To do this, visit retropie.org.uk/download, and from there, you are able to pick out the version of the Raspberry device that you want to work with.

Give it some time to copy over to your SD card.

Once everything is over on the SD card, you can turn on the Raspberry device.

Add in the controller and plug the device into the television while you wait for it to load up.

Add the SD card into the device and give it a few minutes to boot up.

If you did the conversion properly, then you should see the EmulationStation come up on the television screen.

As we start to work on this step, and we get something to show up on the screen, we can then go through and make sure that any and all of the configurations that are necessary here are going to be complete.

The controller is often going to be the best way to handle this because it can make things easier.

And when we work on the controller, it is possible just to go through and click on only the things that we need before finishing it all up.

The first time that we do this is going to take a bit of time because we have never done it before, but the more times we have to go through it, the faster the project will go.

After we have been able to go through and get the Wi-Fi hooked up and ready to go to our device, and you are certain that you have gotten it started up and ready to go, then it is time to add on the ROMS part to this device as well.

Getting this setup and running is going to take a few moments, but the process is simple and pretty similar to what we did before.

To do this, we either need to make sure that we have a nice strong internet connection, or we can use an Ethernet cord.

If your connection is not strong, and the ROMs get interrupted, then you will end up with some messy problems to try and fix.

It is your choice, but often it is best to at least do this part with the Ethernet cord to prevent issues.

Go onto your main computer.

If you are using a Windows computer, you can open up the file manager on the computer and type in a simple code of *"//retropie"*.

If you are working with a Mac computer, you can go to the finder on the computer, select Go, and then click on Connect to Server.

You would then type in the code *"smb://retropie"*.

Both of these end up with the same results—they just have to be done a bit differently on different computers.

At this point, we should have the Wi-Fi and other parts connected properly, and that is when we are going to be able to handle the ROMS over on our device.

We should do this in a remote manner, so that means that we can use the SD card to move our chosen games over, or we are able to choose which games we are going to use the most often and have those get put directly on the Raspberry Pi device.

When you have them transferred through either method, then it is time to start playing!

Turning the Device Into a Phone

The second project that we are able to spend some time on is turning our Raspberry Pi device into a phone.

This is actually easier to do than it may seem, though we have to keep in mind that it is not going to be the most advanced phone.

We will not be creating a phone like a smartphone or anything like that, but it will be able to send and receive calls and even do some basic texting, which can be pretty cool.

To get started with this one, we need to make sure that we have the right tools, and those include:

- Headphones
- Microphone
- An electrical switch
- Velcro squares to help hook it all together
- A touch screen
- GSM module that has an antenna and some audio outlets
- Battery pack to help power the phone
- A Raspberry Pi 3 that can handle the Python coding language

- Duct tape
- Cables
- Zip ties
- A sim card
- A converter for DC-DC
- A foam board that you are able to cut down to be the same size as the Raspberry Pi

When you are picking out the supplies that you need for this project, you should double-check that they are going to be compatible with the Pi 3 and not one of the other versions of Raspberry Pi.

There are a lot of choices out there in terms of the supplies that you can use, and many of them come in at a lower price.

But you want to make sure that they are of high-enough quality, and that they are actually going to work with the device that you want to use.

After we make sure that we have all of the right supplies that will work with our Raspberry Pi device, it is time to make sure that the software we need is put on the device as well.

For this to work, we need to bring in that Python that we talked about earlier, so make sure that this language has been added to our Raspberry Pi device as well.

While we are in this process, we need to make sure that we add on a few other types of software as well, including PiPhone and the WireHunt, so that it will be easier to turn this simple board into the phone that we want to use.

The easiest way for us to add these pieces of software to our device is to add them to the SD card we want to use first and then just transferring those over at a time.

Now that all of these items are present and ready to go, it is time for us to start turning the device into a phone that we are able to use.

The first step to doing this is to connect our battery so that the board, or our phone, will be able to start up.

We need to do this over a switch so the battery ends up with the necessary power.

Once we have this done, it is time to hook both of these to the GSM module.

Take the header of the GSM and then connect it over to the converter that you are using as well.

Once we have been able to go and connect all of these together, it is now time to hook them up to the Raspberry Pi device that we want to work with. We are able to use this with some of the other cables that you should have.

The first part of all of this is to connect the device with the other transmit pins to ensure that they are going to stay with one another.

Check that the pins are all connected to the T and the Rx ports.

While this is going to require us to connect quite a few parts together, once we get this done, and can work with the SIM card, then we are good to go.

Now that all of our lines have had time to be connected and our SIMs card is actually in place, it is now time for us to go and actually assemble all of the parts.

To make sure that this is going to work, we need to bring out that piece of foam that is on our list, and then slice it to be the same size as our Pi device.

Place the device over this piece of foam and then use the squares of Velcro and some duct tape to get the two parts to be together.

This step is important because it is going to help us to connect the converter, the switch, and the module to the other side of our piece of foam you have to make sure that when you add on the battery pack that it goes to a place that is safe, usually somewhere between the Pi device and the screen.

You do not want to have it so that the battery pack is going to move around and cause some trouble.

If it moves around, then the phone will turn off randomly and cause issues along the way.

At this point, if you actually went and connected all of the parts in the proper manner, then you should notice that our phone is going to be done for the most part here, and you should be able to turn it on and get it to actually work.

To turn on the phone, you can just turn on the switch that goes to it, and it should turn on.

From here, you can wait for it to turn on and boot up before dialing any number that you want and use this to make a simple phone call to someone else.

As we can imagine here, this is going to be a pretty simple kind of phone to work with.

We just set it up to do some simple processes, and it is not going to be all that complicated or have any of the features that we want or are used to with some of the other phones that we may have used in the past.

But we are able to use this basic phone to help us make and then receive the codes that we would like, just like a regular phone.

The neat thing is that we can take this a bit further if we would like.

For this project, we are just keeping it simple with a phone that can make and receive the calls that we want.

But it is possible to take this simple phone and set it up to do some other options, like texting and even getting online and so much more.

This just goes to prove that the Raspberry Pi is able to take on a lot of diverse processes if you would like, and it can even, with a few simple steps, go enough to help us to make our own phones.

While we only had time to go through and work on two projects in this chapter, you can see that there is a lot of versatility that we are able to enjoy when it comes to using the Raspberry Pi device.

It is simple to use, and with just a few, and inexpensive accessories, we are able to do so much.

We can use it to create an arcade game to play some of our old favorite games anywhere we go, and even help us make calls with our own phone that we can make.

And there are so many other projects that we are able to do with the same idea, and a few different attachments, along the way.

Conclusion

Thank you for making it through to the end of **Raspberry Pi**, let's hope it was informative and able to provide you with all of the tools you need to achieve your goals whatever they may be.

The next step is to start working with the Raspberry Pi device for your own needs.

There are a lot of neat things that we are able to do when it comes to using the Raspberry Pi, and you are only limited by your knowledge of programming (which the Raspberry Pi device is going to help improve), and your own imagination.

This is the perfect tool for anyone who wants to be able to learn how to program and do some neat things with technology, but who also be a bit scared to jump in because their knowledge is limited.

This guidebook took some time to look more closely at all of the different things that we are able to do when it comes to using the Raspberry Pi device for some of our own needs.

We looked at what this device is all about and some of the benefits that we can enjoy when we use this device for programming.

And we even looked at how to get it connected to some of the other parts that you need, such as USB drives, Wi-Fi, and more so that we are able to actually create some of the projects that we want.

In addition, we took a look at some of the different programming things that we need to keep in mind when we go through this process.

We focused on the Python language and some of the coding that we can do with it.

It is a simple coding language that we can learn as a beginner, and you will find that it is one of the best options to help you out when it is time to work on the Raspberry Pi, along with many other options for coding along the way.

There are a lot of different things that we are able to do when it comes to using the Raspberry Pi device, and you will find that this is the perfect device to help us get going with programming, especially if we are an absolute beginner.

When you are ready to get started with programming with the Raspberry Pi, and learning how to do some of your own programming in Python, make sure to check out this guidebook to get started.

Finally, if you found this book useful in any way, a review on Amazon is always appreciated!

www.ingramcontent.com/pod-product-compliance
Lightning Source LLC
Chambersburg PA
CBHW071411210526
45465CB00001B/333